DEVOPS EXPLAINED WITH EASE

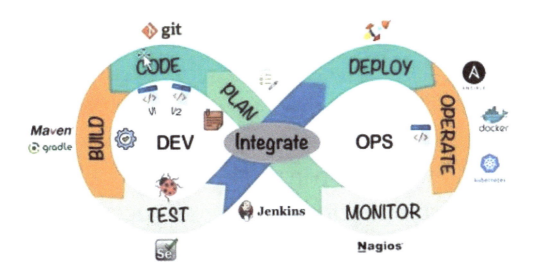

Learn Cloud, Linux, Git, Docker, and CI/CD the Easy Way

Basil U

Cover Design by Basil U

Disclaimer: The information in this book is provided "as is," without any guarantees of completeness, accuracy, or results obtained from the use of this information. Readers are encouraged to adapt techniques to their unique circumstances.

About Author

Basil U. is a passionate DevOps engineer, cloud enthusiast, and tech educator dedicated to making complex topics simple and practical.

With hands-on experience across Linux systems, AWS cloud services, Git version control, Docker containers, Terraform automation, and CI/CD pipelines, Basil U. has helped countless aspiring engineers and IT professionals build real-world DevOps skills from scratch.

Starting from humble beginnings with basic server setups and scripting, Basil U. understands what it feels like to be overwhelmed, and that's why this book is built on clear explanations, step-by-step tutorials, and practical exercises that anyone can follow.

When not deploying cloud infrastructure or automating workflows, Basil U. enjoys mentoring newcomers to tech, sharing real-world DevOps tips, and continually learning the latest tools and trends in the DevOps world.

Basil U. believes:
"Anyone can master DevOps, if you learn it the easy, practical way.". Follow Basil U. for more tech tips, free resources, and updates.

Preface

Welcome!

When I first started learning DevOps, it felt overwhelming. So many tools. So many cloud services. So many commands. I constantly asked myself, Where do I even begin?
If you're feeling the same way, you're not alone, and you're exactly who I wrote this book for.

DevOps Explained With Ease was born from a simple idea:

Make DevOps simple, practical, and beginner-friendly.
This book is designed to be your hands-on guide.

You'll go beyond just reading, you'll build, automate, deploy, and troubleshoot real world projects step by step.
Inside, you'll find:

Inside, you'll find:

- Clear, easy to follow explanations without jargon
- Practical exercises you can do at home, even with a basic laptop
- Real world workflows that real DevOps engineers use every day
- Projects that help you practice, not just memorize

You'll start with fundamentals like launching your first server, mastering Linux basics, and working with Git. Then we'll level up, building containers with Docker, automating infrastructure with Terraform, setting up CI/CD pipelines, and even monitoring and securing your deployments.

By the time you finish this book, you'll not only understand DevOps you'll be doing DevOps.
Whether you're aiming to land your first tech job, upskill for a better role, or just explore this exciting field, you are taking an amazing first step.

I'm so excited to be part of your journey.
Let's dive in and start building!
Basil U.
Author of DevOps Explained With Ease

Content

Content

Content

Content

Introduction

Introduction. Your DevOps Journey Begins Here

Welcome to DevOps Explained With Ease!

If you're holding this book, you're likely curious, excited, maybe a little overwhelmed, and that's exactly how every DevOps engineer starts. Trust me, you're in the right place.

What Is DevOps?

At its heart, DevOps is about bridging the gap between developers and operations.

It's about building, testing, releasing, and maintaining software faster, more reliably, and more securely, by combining the power of automation, cloud technologies, and smart collaboration.

In short:

DevOps makes software delivery smoother, faster, and better.

Why DevOps Matters (More Than Ever)

In today's digital world, companies expect apps, websites, and services to update frequently, without downtime or chaos.

That's why DevOps professionals are in huge demand, and why learning DevOps can launch your tech career to the next level.

Companies like Amazon, Netflix, and Google all rely heavily on DevOps principles to stay ahead.
You can too.

Companies like Amazon, Netflix, and Google all rely heavily on DevOps principles to stay ahead.
You can too.

How This Book Will Help You

This is not just a theory book.
This is a hands-on guide designed to give you:

- Real world skills (not just memorized commands)
- Confidence working with servers, cloud platforms, and automation tools
- Step by step projects you can put on your resume or portfolio
- Foundations that prepare you for professional DevOps certifications and jobs

You'll build real projects using:

- AWS EC2, S3, IAM, VPC, CloudWatch
- Linux Shell Scripting, File and Folder Operations, Automation
- Git & GitHub for version control and collaboration
- Docker for containerization
- Terraform for Infrastructure as Code
- CI/CD Pipelines using Jenkins and GitHub Actions
- Ansible for server configuration

By the end of this book, you won't just know DevOps – you'll live it.

Who This Book Is For

- Beginners curious about DevOps
- Developers wanting to expand into cloud and automation
- Sysadmins upgrading their skills
- Anyone aiming for a cloud, DevOps, or Site Reliability Engineer (SRE) role

What You Need

- A computer (Windows, macOS, or Linux)
- Internet access
- A willingness to get your hands dirty and try things out!

Don't worry if you don't know AWS, Git, or Linux yet.

I'll guide you every step of the way, explaining what, why, and how without confusing tech jargon.

A Quick Word Before We Begin
 The tech world moves fast.
 But you don't have to master everything at once.
 DevOps is a journey, and this book is your map.
Ready to start building, deploying, and mastering DevOps?
Let's dive in.

⬤ Why This Works:

- Super easy to understand, no intimidating jargon ▪
- Clearly explains the "why" behind DevOps ▪
- Focuses on practical, real world results ▪
- Inspires beginners to keep reading and learning ▪
- Sets expectations so readers know exactly what they'll achieve ▪

Chapter 1

Getting Started with DevOps Basics

What is DevOps?
Before we jump into the exciting hands-on parts, let's first answer a basic but important question:

What exactly is DevOps?

At its core, DevOps is a combination of two words:
- Dev = Development
- Ops = Operations

It's a set of practices and tools designed to bridge the gap between software developers and IT operations teams

Instead of working in silos, both teams collaborate closely, to build, test, and release software faster, more reliably, and more securely.

Think of DevOps as a culture of continuous improvement where:
- Developers don't just write code and throw it over the wall to operations.
- Operations teams don't just manage servers without understanding the applications they run.

Instead, everyone works together, with shared responsibilities, better automation, and faster delivery cycles.

Why does DevOps matter?

- Faster deployments
- Fewer bugs and outages
- Happier users and customers
- More secure and scalable systems
- Stronger collaboration between teams

In today's fast paced tech world, companies that adopt DevOps move faster and win more customers, and that's why DevOps engineers are in huge demand.

Category	Examples	Purpose
Version Control	Git, GitHub, GitLab	Track code changes
Containerization	Docker, Kubernetes	Package apps into containers
Cloud Providers	AWS, Azure, Google Cloud	Host servers and applications
CI/CD (Automation)	Jenkins, GitHub Actions, GitLab CI	Automate build, test, deployment
Infrastructure as Code	Terraform, AWS CloudFormation	Manage servers & networks as code
Configuration Management	Ansible, Chef, Puppet	Automate software setup and configuration
Monitoring & Logging	CloudWatch, Prometheus, ELK Stack	Track system health and troubleshoot issues

Don't worry you don't need to learn all of them at once!
In this book, we'll focus on the most essential and beginner–friendly tools that give you the fastest results.

You'll start with:
- AWS EC2 (virtual servers in the cloud)
- PuTTY & PuTTYgen (connecting to your server)
- Linux Shell Basics (essential commands to control your server)
- Git (version control to manage code)

These are your first building blocks toward becoming a confident DevOps engineer

Setting Up Your DevOps Lab

(EC2, PuTTY, Linux Basics)

Learning by doing is the fastest way to master DevOps.

That's why we're going to set up a personal DevOps Lab where you can safely practice without risking real world systems.

Here's what you'll need:

◼ An AWS Free Tier Account:
Amazon Web Services (AWS) offers free access to basic cloud resources, including virtual servers (called EC2 instances). You'll sign up and launch your very first cloud server.

■ PuTTY and PuTTYgen:

PuTTY is a free SSH client that lets you connect securely to your Linux server.
PuTTYgen helps generate the necessary private keys.

■ Basic Linux Knowledge:

You'll learn essential Linux commands to:
- Navigate files and folders
- Edit files using vi mode
- Manage users and permissions
- Automate tasks with shell scripts

Mini Project 1: Your First Cloud Server

In the next chapter, you'll:
- Launch your first EC2 server
- Connect to it using PuTTY
- Run your first Linux commands
- 🙂 Hands-on and simple, even if you've never touched a server before!

🟦 Your First Cloud Server

Step 1: Create an AWS Account

1. Visit https://aws.amazon.com/.
2. Click Create an AWS Account.
3. Fill in your email address, password, and payment information (AWS Free Tier requires a card but won't charge unless you go beyond free limits).
4. Choose Personal account (for learning).
5. Complete identity verification via phone and email.

⬛ Done! You now have an AWS account.

Step 2: Launch an EC2 Instance (Virtual Server)

1. Log in to your AWS Management Console.
2. In the search bar at the top, type EC2 and click it.
3. Click Launch Instance (big orange button).
4. Fill out the form:
   - Name: Give your instance a friendly name like MyFirstServer.
   - Amazon Machine Image (AMI): Choose Amazon Linux 2 (free tier eligible).
   - Instance Type: Choose t2.micro (free tier eligible).
   - Key Pair (Login):
     - Click Create new key pair.
     - Name it something like mykey.
     - Key pair type: RSA
     - Private key file format: .pem
     - Download and save the .pem file safely , you'll need it!
   - Network settings: Allow SSH (port 22) from My IP.
   - Leave storage settings as default.
5. Click Launch Instance.

Congratulations! Your cloud server (EC2 instance) is now running!

Login at AWS Console

IAM user sign in ⓘ

Account ID or alias (Don't have?)

☐ Remember this account

IAM username

Password

☐ Show Password   Having trouble?

Sign in

Sign in using root user email

Create a new AWS account

---

aws

Free, on-demand training

Boost your career with
600+ digital courses on
AWS Skill Builder

Learn more >

Click on sign in as root user or use email instead
You should see something like this if successfully log In

Step 3: Convert the .pem Key to .ppk Using PuTTYgen

PuTTY (Windows SSH client) needs a .ppk file instead of .pem.

Let's convert it.
1. Open PuTTYgen (install it if you haven't yet, it's free).
2. Click Load.
3. Change the file type to All Files (*.*).
4. Locate and open your downloaded .pem file.
5. Click Save Private Key (you can skip the passphrase warning for now).
6. Save it as something like mykey.ppk.

◼ Done! You now have the private key PuTTY can use.

Step 4: Connect to Your EC2 Instance Using PuTTY

1. Open PuTTY.
2. In the Host Name field, enter:
3. ec2-user@your-public-ip-address
4. (Find your EC2 instance's Public IPv4 address in the AWS console.)
5. In the left menu, under Connection > SSH > Auth, browse and select your .ppk private key.
6. Click Open.
7. A security alert may pop up, click Yes.

Boom! You're now logged into your Linux server!

Launch PuTTygen, Click on Load

PuTTY Key Generator

File   Key   Conversions   Help

Key

Public key for pasting into OpenSSH authorized_keys file:

```
ssh-rsa
AAAAB3NzaC1yc2EAAAADAQABAAABAQDK8xI............        .60BxgBnxRahOca//oKKdQIEG
H/bFP/g8BPuxvhCOu8lmiPS- '+HrDawrUUcB7OodN70XKgwfYspqKPd140uzHg7F3JN+Vw7VnSJXCdWT
+nl8xG5M..                ..RFPmizyTUI4v765edjeDmGyhdq6b6ufWLgX0O2JFn115z4oj/ogsLpdbRvYaj
QSeA1oZl9wgvf7fjlevKUoPPEUIxKsytcbOiDDjrctPbW~ ~~        ............ ...R
```

Key fingerprint:	ssh-rsa `2··` 3HA256:0FUPnjhFpap+WnVue9r+5S. ..
Key comment:	imported-openssh-key
Key passphrase:	
Confirm passphrase:	

Actions

Generate a public/private key pair		Generate
Load an existing private key file		Load
Save the generated key	Save public key	Save private key

Parameters

Type of key to generate:
( ) RSA   ( ) DSA   ( ) ECDSA   ( ) EdDSA   ( ) SSH-1 (RSA)

Number of bits in a generated key: 2048

Select All Files

PuTTY Private Key Files (*.ppk)

| PuTTY Private Key Files (*.ppk) |
| All Files (*.*) |

Select All Files

Select the .pem file you downloaded and open it

Click on Save as Private key, then click Yes

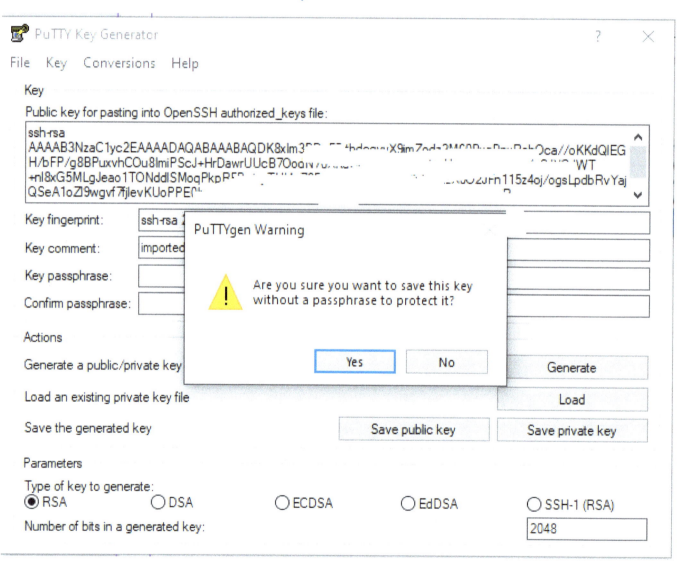

Save the file with name you can remember

Launch PuTTy, Enter your public IP Address

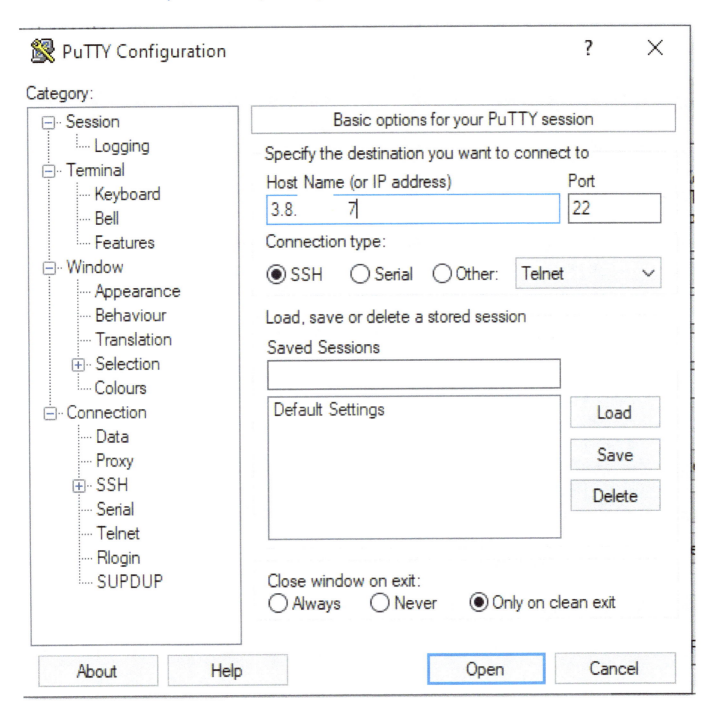

In the left menu, under Connection > SSH > Auth, browse and select your .ppk private key.

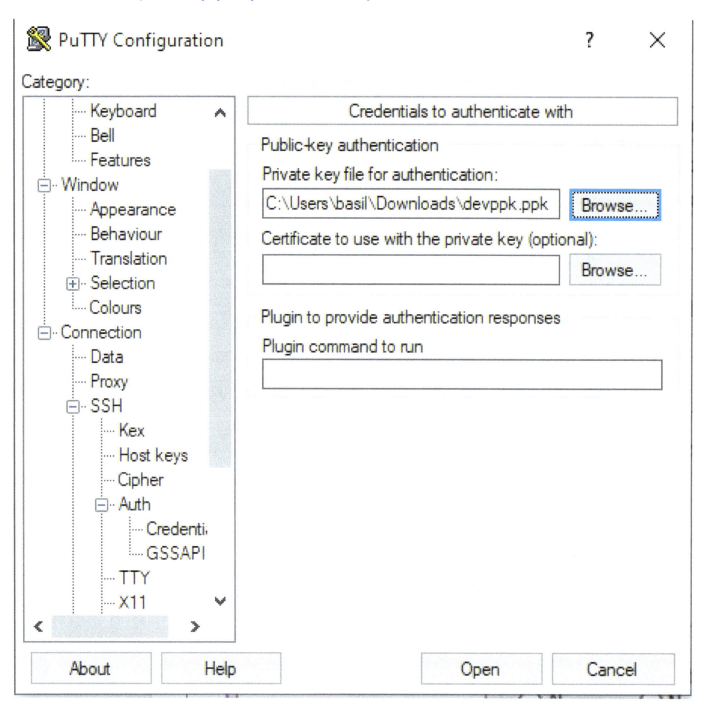

In the left menu, under Connection > SSH > Auth, browse
and select your .ppk private key.

Step 5: Run Your First Linux Commands

In the black terminal window (your EC2 server):
Try typing:

```bash
whoami
```

(Shows the current user. You should see `ec2-user`.)

```bash
pwd
```

(Shows your present working directory — likely `/home/ec2-user`.)

```bash
ls
```

(Lists files and folders.)

```bash
uptime
```

You just successfully:
- Created a real cloud server
- Connected securely to it
- Ran your first Linux commands

Try creating a folder and a file on your server:

mkdir myfolder
cd myfolder
echo "Hello DevOps!" > hello.txt
cat hello.txt

Chapter 2

Core Linux and Shell Scripting Skills

4. Linux Command Line Mastery

The Linux command line (also called shell) is where you'll spend a lot of your time as a DevOps engineer. It may look intimidating at first, but trust us, once you get the hang of it, it's a powerful and efficient tool that will make your DevOps life easier.

Here's how to master the basics:

file_viewing_and_manipulation.sh

Release Notes: 1.99.3 $ devmi.sh ✕

$ devmi.sh

```bash
 1    #!/bin/bash
 2
 3    # Basic Navigation Commands
 4    # pwd — Print the current directory.
 5    pwd
 6
 7    # ls — List the contents of a directory.
 8    ls
 9
10    # cd — Change directory.
11    mkdir devopsspace
12
13    # cd — Change directory.
14    cd devopsspace/
15
16    # clear — Clear the terminal screen.
17    clear
```

PROBLEMS   OUTPUT   DEBUG CONSOLE   TERMINAL   PORTS   GITLENS

○ [ec2-user@ip-172-31.   ]$ ▯

$ devmi.sh

```bash
1    #!/bin/bash
2
3    # File Viewing Commands Demo
4
5    echo "➡ Creating a sample file for viewing..."
6    echo "This is a sample file for testing file viewing commands." > samplefile.txt
7
8    echo ""
9    echo "➡ Viewing the contents of the file using cat:"
10   cat samplefile.txt
11
12   echo ""
13   echo "➡ Viewing the file one page at a time using more:"
14   more samplefile.txt
15
16   echo ""
17   echo "➡ Viewing the file with scrolling features using less (press q to quit):"
18   less samplefile.txt
19
```

file_and_folder_operations.sh

```bash
$ devmi.sh
1    #!/bin/bash
2
3    # File Manipulation Commands
4
5    echo ""
6    echo "➡️ Creating a new empty file 'newfile.txt'..."
7    touch newfile.txt
8    ls -l newfile.txt
9
10   echo ""
11   echo "➡️ Copying 'newfile.txt' to 'copy_of_newfile.txt'..."
12   cp newfile.txt copy_of_newfile.txt
13   ls -l copy_of_newfile.txt
14
15   echo ""
16   echo "➡️ Moving 'copy_of_newfile.txt' to 'moved_newfile.txt'..."
17   mv copy_of_newfile.txt moved_newfile.txt
18   ls -l moved_newfile.txt
19
20   echo ""
21   echo "➡️ Removing 'moved_newfile.txt'..."
22   rm moved_newfile.txt
23   ls -l || echo "✅ File removed successfully."
24
25   echo ""
26   echo "➡️ Creating and removing a directory:"
27   mkdir temp_folder
28   ls -ld temp_folder
29   rmdir temp_folder
30   ls -ld temp_folder || echo "✅ Folder removed successfully."
31
```

```bash
1    #!/bin/bash
2
3    # File and Folder Operations Demo
4
5    echo "→ Creating a new directory 'myfolder'..."
6    mkdir myfolder
7    ls -ld myfolder
8
9    echo ""
10   echo "→ Listing files and folders in long format:"
11   ls -l
12
13   echo ""
14   echo "→ Listing all files, including hidden ones:"
15   ls -a
16
17   echo ""
18   echo "→ Creating a test file 'oldfilename.txt' inside 'myfolder'..."
19   touch myfolder/oldfilename.txt
20   ls -l myfolder/
21
22   echo ""
23   echo "→ Renaming 'oldfilename.txt' to 'newfilename.txt'..."
24   mv myfolder/oldfilename.txt myfolder/newfilename.txt
25   ls -l myfolder/
26
27   echo ""
28   echo "→ Copying 'myfolder' to 'backup_folder'..."
29   cp -r myfolder backup_folder
30   ls -l
31
```

first_shell_script.sh script

```bash
#!/bin/bash

# My First Shell Script

echo "Hello, DevOps!"
echo ""
echo "Listing files in the current directory:"
ls -l
```

After typing the script use control + d to go out
use chmod +x first_shell_script.sh to grant execution
then in your terminal type

```
chmod +x first_shell_script.sh
./first_shell_script.sh
```

first_shell_script.sh with puTTY

```
[ec2-user@ip-172-3          ~]$ cat > first_shell_script.sh
echo "Hello, World"
echo ""
echo "Listing Filees in the Current Directories"
ls -l
[ec2-user@ip-172-3          ~]$ chmod +x first_shell_script.sh
[ec2-user@ip-172-3          ~]$ ./first_shell_script.sh
Hello, World

Listing Filees in the Current Directories
total 88
drwxrwxr-x. 2 ec2-user ec2-user     6 Apr  7 10:37 anotherfolder
drwxrwxr-x. 3 ec2-user ec2-user   148 Apr 19 19:13 backup
-rwxrwxr-x. 1 ec2-user ec2-user   886 Apr  6 17:44 basilfileopr.sh
-rwxrwxr-x. 1 ec2-user ec2-user  1979 Apr  5 18:27 bkscript.sh
-rwxrwxr-x. 1 ec2-user ec2-user  1032 Apr  5 21:49 bktut.sh
-rwxrwxr-x. 1 ec2-user ec2-user   260 Apr  5 19:37 bracketsuse.sh
-rw-rw-r--. 1 ec2-user ec2-user   765 Apr 13 05:19 car_speed.sh
-rwxrwxr-x. 1 ec2-user ec2-user    19 Apr 19 18:01 devma.sh
-rw-rw-r--. 1 ec2-user ec2-user     0 Apr 12 18:17 devme.sh
-rw-rw-r--. 1 ec2-user ec2-user    19 Apr 13 05:52 devme.txt
-rwxrwxr-x. 1 ec2-user ec2-user   266 Apr 20 09:54 devmi.sh
drwxrwxr-x. 2 ec2-user ec2-user     6 Apr 20 09:52 devopsspace
-rw-rw-r--. 1 ec2-user ec2-user   312 Apr 13 05:34 diffscript.sh
-rwxrwxr-x. 1 ec2-user ec2-user   354 Apr  7 10:18 evennumbers.sh
-rw-rw-r--. 1 ec2-user ec2-user    53 Apr 13 06:14 exploreeof.sh
-rw-rw-r--. 1 ec2-user ec2-user    19 Apr 13 05:38 file.txt
-rwxr-xr-x. 1 ec2-user ec2-user    83 Apr 20 10:43 first_shell_script.sh
-rwxrwxr-x. 1 ec2-user ec2-user   429 Apr  6 19:00 forloop.sh
drwxrwxr-x. 5 ec2-user ec2-user   142 Apr 19 21:22 gitspace
-rwxrwxr-x. 1 ec2-user ec2-user   368 Apr  5 21:20 john
drwxrwxr-x. 2 ec2-user ec2-user     6 Apr  5 21:12 johnfolder
drwxrwxr-x. 2 ec2-user ec2-user    41 Apr  5 21:50 johntut
-rw-rw-r--. 1 ec2-user ec2-user   815 Apr 13 05:52 metachar.sh
-rwxrwxr-x. 1 ec2-user ec2-user   328 Apr  5 21:04 multiplecase.sh
-rw-rw-r--. 1 ec2-user ec2-user    83 Apr  5 20:49 multiplecasepattern.sh
-rwxrwxr-x. 1 ec2-user ec2-user   386 Apr  5 18:23 script.sh
-rwxrwxr-x. 1 ec2-user ec2-user  1129 Apr 13 18:18 scriptsat.sh
-rwxrwxr-x. 1 ec2-user ec2-user   368 Apr  5 18:59 shellloop.sh
-rw-rw-r--. 1 ec2-user ec2-user     0 Apr 12 18:27 test
-rwxrwxr-x. 1 ec2-user ec2-user   105 Apr  7 10:38 variablesub.sh
[ec2-user@ip-172           ~]$
```

📄 loops_and_decision_making.sh

☰ Release Notes: 1.99.3 $ devmi.sh ⬤   ☰ config

$ devmi.sh

```bash
1   #!/bin/bash
2
3   # Loops and Decision-Making Demo
4
5   echo "🔵 For loop demo:"
6   for i in {1..5}
7   do
8   |   echo "Iteration number $i"
9   done
10
11  echo ""
12  echo "🔵 While loop demo:"
13  counter=1
14  while [ $counter -le 5 ]
15  do
16  |   echo "Counter is $counter"
17  |   ((counter++))
18  done
19
20  echo ""
21  echo "🔵 If-Else Decision Making Demo:"
22  if [ -f "checkfile.txt" ]; then
23  |   echo "✅ checkfile.txt exists."
24  else
25  |   echo "❌ checkfile.txt does not exist."
26  fi
27
```

loops_and_decision_making.sh

```
28    echo ""
29    echo "🔁 Automation with loop and if-check:"
30    for file in *.txt
31    do
32      if [ -f "$file" ]; then
33        echo "Processing file: $file"
34        # You can add commands like cat $file or mv $file somewhere else here
35      fi
36    done
37
```

Chapter 3

Version Control with Git

Mastering Git for DevOps Success

In the world of DevOps, version control isn't optional – it's essential.

Think of Git as the backbone of modern software development.

Without it, projects would be chaos.

In this chapter, you'll learn:
- What Git is and why it matters
- How to connect your local Visual Studio Code (VSCode) to an EC2 instance
- Real-world Git workflows: push, pull, merge, and more
- Hands-on exercises to make you Git-proficient

Let's get started.

Git Essentials for DevOps

What is Git?

Git is a version control system that helps you track changes in your code over time.

It allows multiple people (or just you!) to:
- Save different versions of a project
- Work on different features without conflict
- Revert to older versions if something breaks
- Collaborate easily across teams

Key Git Concepts:

- Repository (Repo): A storage space for your project's code.
- Commit: A snapshot of your project at a particular moment.
- Branch: A separate line of development.
- Merge: Combining different branches into one.
- Push: Uploading changes from your local machine to a remote server (like GitHub).
- Pull: Downloading changes from a remote server to your local machine.

DevOps Reality Check:

Almost every DevOps pipeline starts with a Git repository. It's the foundation for Continuous Integration (CI) and Continuous Deployment (CD).

Setting Up Git Locally

Before we connect anything to AWS, let's make sure Git is installed locally.

⬛ Install Git:

Windows: <u>Download Git for Windows</u>

Mac:

Open Terminal and run:

- brew install git

Linux:

Open Terminal and run:

- sudo apt-get install git

⬛ Configure Git (First Time Only):

git config --global user.name "Your Name"
git config --global user.email "youremail@example.com"

🔗 Connecting Local VSCode to EC2 with Git

Step 1: SSH into EC2 from VSCode
Install the Remote – SSH extension in VSCode.
Then in the Command Palette (Ctrl+Shift+P), search for Remote-SSH: Connect to Host... and connect to your EC2 instance using your .pem file.

Or if you prefer the traditional way:
Open a terminal inside VSCode and connect:

```
ssh -i your-key.pem ec2-user@your-ec2-ip-address
```

Step 2: Install Git on the EC2 Instance
If it's not installed yet:

```
sudo yum install git -y
```
or
```
sudo apt-get install git -y
```

(Depending on whether your EC2 is Amazon Linux, Ubuntu, etc.)

Step 3: Initialize a Git Repository on EC2

git init

Step 4: Set Up Remote Access (Optional Advanced)

You can connect your EC2 repo to GitHub or Bitbucket later to back up your server-side code automatically. We'll cover that later in CI/CD.

Real-World Git Workflow (Push, Pull, Merge)

Now, let's walk through a practical DevOps Git flow.

1. Create a Local Project
On your local machine:

```
mkdir my-devops-project
cd my-devops-project
git init
```

Create a simple file:

```
echo "Hello DevOps!" > readme.txt
```

2. Track and Commit Changes

```
git add .
git commit -m "Initial commit – DevOps project setup"
```

3. Connect to a Remote Repository

First, create a new repository on GitHub.
 Then link it:

```
git remote add origin https://github.com/your-username/your-repo-name.git
```

4. Push Local Code to Remote

```
git push -u origin master
```
■ Now your code is safely stored on GitHub!

5. Pull Changes From Remote

When you (or your teammates) make changes and you want to sync:

```
git pull origin master
```

6. Working with Branches
Create a branch for a new feature:

git checkout -b feature-login-page

Work on your changes, commit them, then push the branch:

git push origin feature-login-page

7. Merge Changes
After review, merge the feature branch into master:

git checkout master
git merge feature-login-page
git push origin master

Pro Tip: Always pull the latest changes before you start working to avoid merge conflicts.

Hands-On Exercise: Git + EC2 Mini Project

- Connect VSCode to your EC2 server.
- Create a simple project on your local machine.
- Initialize Git, commit code, push to GitHub.
- Pull the same code down to your EC2 instance.
- Update a file on EC2, commit the change, and push it back to GitHub.

This practice will teach you the real DevOps cycle that happens thousands of times a day in companies all over the world.

Chapter 4

Hands-on Cloud Computing with AWS

Welcome to the cloud!

In this chapter, we're getting hands-on with the world's leading cloud platform – Amazon Web Services (AWS).
If you've ever wondered how companies manage thousands of servers without owning physical hardware, you're about to learn.

With AWS, you can build, deploy, and scale powerful infrastructure – all from your laptop.
Let's get started!

Deep Dive into EC2 Management

What is EC2?

Amazon Elastic Compute Cloud (EC2) lets you create virtual servers – called instances – in minutes.
Instead of buying physical hardware, you simply launch a server in the cloud.

Practical: Launching Your First EC2 Instance

1. Log into your AWS Management Console.
2. Go to EC2 > Launch Instance.
3. Choose an Amazon Machine Image (AMI) (e.g., Amazon Linux 2).
4. Select an instance type (t2.micro for free tier).
5. Configure security groups to allow SSH (port 22).
6. Generate and download a key pair (.pem file) – this will be used to connect.
7. Launch your instance!

Connecting to EC2 with PuTTY

If you're using Windows:
- Convert your .pem file to .ppk format using PuTTYgen.
- Use PuTTY to SSH into your instance.

Sample Linux Commands Once Connected:

sudo yum update –y
sudo yum install git –y

You are now managing a cloud server – congrats!

Working with S3: Buckets, Uploads, Permissions
What is S3?

Simple Storage Service (S3) lets you store and retrieve files easily and securely.
Think of it like Dropbox, but for cloud applications.

Practical: Create a Bucket and Upload a File
1. Go to S3 > Create Bucket.
2. Name your bucket (e.g., devops-demo-bucket) — names must be globally unique!
3. Set region, block public access for now.
4. After creating, upload a file (like a test .txt file).

Setting Permissions
- Manage who can view or edit your files.
- Use Bucket Policies or Access Control Lists (ACLs) for fine-grained control.

Pro Tip: Enable Versioning to keep old copies of files automatically.

Mastering IAM: Users, Roles, Policies

What is IAM?

Identity and Access Management (IAM) controls who can do what in your AWS account.
Never use your root account for daily work — use IAM users!

Practical: Create a User with Limited Permissions

1. Go to IAM > Users > Add User.
2. Create a user with programmatic access (for CLI) and/or console access.
3. Attach a policy (like AmazonS3ReadOnlyAccess).

Understanding IAM Components

- Users: Specific people or apps.
- Groups: Collection of users.
- Roles: Temporary access to resources (great for EC2 instances).
- Policies: JSON documents that define permissions.

Example: A Policy to Allow EC2 Access

```json
{
    "Version": "2012-10-17",
    "Statement": [
        {
            "Effect": "Allow",
            "Action": "ec2:*",
            "Resource": "*"
        }
    ]
}
```

Introduction to VPC and Networking

What is VPC?

Virtual Private Cloud (VPC) is your private network inside AWS.
Think of it like your own data center with full control over networking.

Key Concepts:
- Subnets: Smaller sections inside a VPC (public/private).
- Route Tables: Rules for traffic direction.
- Internet Gateway: Allows internet access.
- Security Groups & NACLs: Firewalls at the instance and subnet levels.

Practical: Set Up a Simple VPC
1. Go to VPC > Create VPC.
2. Add subnets (one public, one private).
3. Attach an internet gateway.
4. Launch an EC2 instance into your new public subnet.

You're now running a server inside your own custom network!

Monitoring with CloudWatch

What is CloudWatch?

AWS CloudWatch monitors your applications and infrastructure – from logs to performance metrics.

You can:

- View CPU, memory, disk usage
- Create alarms for thresholds
- Set automated actions (like scaling up servers!)

Practical: Create a CPU Alarm

1. Go to CloudWatch > Alarms > Create Alarm.
2. Choose a metric (e.g., CPU Utilization for your EC2).
3. Set threshold (e.g., > 80% CPU usage).
4. Configure notification via SNS (Simple Notification Service).

Bonus: Install the CloudWatch Agent on EC2 to monitor memory and disk space too.

Summary

By now, you've:
- Launched and connected to EC2 servers
- Stored and managed files with S3
- Secured your account with IAM
- Built private cloud networks with VPC
- Monitored your systems with CloudWatch

You're officially working hands-on in the cloud like a real DevOps engineer!

In the next chapters, we'll level up by learning Docker, Infrastructure as Code with Terraform, and setting up automation pipelines!

Get ready — things are about to get even more exciting!

Chapter 5

Containers and Infrastructure as Code

Introduction to Docker and Containers

Imagine if you could package your entire app – the code, the settings, the system libraries – into one neat box that runs exactly the same anywhere.

That's what containers do!

Docker is the most popular tool for creating and managing containers.

It solves the old "but it worked on my machine!" problem by making sure your app behaves the same way on your laptop, your server, or even in the cloud.

Key Idea:

Containers = Lightweight, portable virtual environments.

Why Use Containers?

- Fast to start
- Consistent environments
- Easy to share and deploy

Building Your First Docker Container

Let's build your very first container – it's easier than you think!

Step 1: Install Docker
Download Docker Desktop for your system (Windows, macOS, or Linux) and install it.

Step 2: Create a Simple App
Let's make a simple HTML web page.
Create a folder called myapp, and inside it create a file named index.html:

```html
<!DOCTYPE html>
<html>
  <head><title>Hello from Docker</title></head>
  <body><h1>It Works!</h1></body>
</html>
```

Step 3: Create a Dockerfile

A Dockerfile tells Docker how to build your container. Inside the myapp folder, create a file called Dockerfile (no extension) with this content:

```
FROM nginx:latest
COPY index.html /usr/share/nginx/html/index.html
```

- FROM nginx:latest   Use the official Nginx web server image.
- COPY   Replace the default web page with your own.

Step 4: Build and Run the Container
Open a terminal, navigate to your myapp folder, and run:

```
docker build -t myfirstdockerapp .
docker run -d -p 8080:80 myfirstdockerapp
```

Then open your browser and visit http://localhost:8080 — boom!
You just built and launched your first container!

Using Docker Compose for Multi-Container Apps

In real-world projects, you often need multiple containers – for example, one for your web app and another for your database.

Docker Compose makes it easy to manage multi-container setups using a simple docker-compose.yml file.

Example: A Web App + Database
Create a docker-compose.yml:

```yaml
version: '3'
services:
  web:
    image: nginx
    ports:
      - "8080:80"
  db:
    image: mysql
    environment:
      MYSQL_ROOT_PASSWORD: examplepassword
```

Run everything with one command:

```
docker-compose up
```

🟦 Now you have two services running together – a web server and a database – without manual setup!

Infrastructure as Code with Terraform

So far, you've manually clicked around AWS to launch instances and services.

What if you could write code that automatically creates your cloud infrastructure?
That's where Infrastructure as Code (IaC) comes in.
Terraform is one of the most powerful IaC tools.
It lets you define your cloud environment in simple text files – and deploy or update it with a single command.

■ Why Use Terraform?
- Automate infrastructure creation
- Version control your infrastructure like code
- Reuse and share configurations easily

Creating AWS Resources with Terraform

Let's create an AWS EC2 instance using Terraform!
Step 1: Install Terraform
Download it from the official site and install it.
Step 2: Create Your Terraform File
Create a file called main.tf with the following:

```
provider "aws" {
  region = "us-east-1"
}

resource "aws_instance" "example" {
  ami         = "ami-0c55b159cbfafe1f0"  # (Ubuntu AMI for your region)
  instance_type = "t2.micro"
}
```

Step 3: Initialize and Apply
In your terminal:

```
terraform init
terraform apply
```

Confirm when prompted, and Terraform will automatically create your EC2 instance!

Congratulations, you've just automated cloud infrastructure!

Chapter 6

Automation, CI/CD, and Configuration Management

n the world of DevOps, automation is the engine that powers speed, reliability, and efficiency.
Instead of manually setting up servers, running tests, or deploying applications each time, we automate these tasks.

This frees up time, reduces human error, and lets teams move faster and more confidently.

In this chapter, you'll discover:
- The fundamentals of CI/CD (Continuous Integration and Continuous Deployment)
- How to build your first Jenkins pipeline
- How to deploy using GitHub Actions
- How to configure servers automatically with Ansible

Let's dive right in!

CI/CD Basics: Concepts and Tools

CI/CD is one of the pillars of modern DevOps.

Here's a simple way to think about it:

- Continuous Integration (CI):
- Every time you (or your team) make a change to the code, it's automatically tested and merged into the shared repository.
- Continuous Deployment (CD):
- Once the code passes tests, it's automatically deployed to servers, so users can access the latest updates without delays.

Why CI/CD Matters:

- Speeds up software delivery
- Reduces bugs and downtime
- Increases developer confidence
- Makes releases boring (in a good way!)

Popular CI/CD Tools:
- Jenkins (open-source and extremely customizable)
- GitHub Actions (great for GitHub-based workflows)
- GitLab CI/CD
- CircleCI
- AWS CodePipeline

In this chapter, we'll focus on two of the most popular tools: Jenkins and GitHub Actions.

Building a Jenkins Pipeline
What is Jenkins?

Jenkins is an open-source automation server that lets you build, test, and deploy applications automatically.

Step 1: Install Jenkins
- Launch an EC2 instance (Ubuntu works well)
- Install Java:

```
sudo apt update
sudo apt install openjdk-11-jdk -y
```

Add Jenkins repository and install:

```
curl -fsSL https://pkg.jenkins.io/debian/jenkins.io-
2023.key | sudo tee \
/usr/share/keyrings/jenkins-keyring.asc > /dev/null

echo deb [signed-by=/usr/share/keyrings/jenkins-
keyring.asc] \
https://pkg.jenkins.io/debian binary/ | sudo tee \
/etc/apt/sources.list.d/jenkins.list > /dev/null

sudo apt update
sudo apt install jenkins -y
```

Start Jenkins:

```
sudo systemctl start jenkins
sudo systemctl enable jenkins
```

Access Jenkins by visiting http://your-ec2-public-ip:8080 in a browser.

Step 2: Set Up a Simple Pipeline

1. Click New Item   Select Pipeline   Give it a name.
2. In the Pipeline section, add this basic script:

```
pipeline {
  agent any

  stages {
    stage('Build') {
      steps {
        echo 'Building the application...'
      }
    }
    stage('Test') {
      steps {
        echo 'Running tests...'
      }
    }
    stage('Deploy') {
      steps {
        echo 'Deploying application...'
      }
    }
  }
}
```

Save and click Build Now — watch the magic happen!

Congrats!
You've just created your first Jenkins pipeline!

Deploying with GitHub Actions
What is GitHub Actions?

GitHub Actions is an automation platform that's built into GitHub.

You can automate your workflows directly from your GitHub repositories!

Why Use GitHub Actions?
- Super easy to set up
- Perfect for small and medium projects
- No extra servers needed (like Jenkins)

How to Set Up a Basic Workflow
1. Inside your GitHub repo, create a folder: .github/workflows
2. Inside it, create a file: main.yml
3. Add this simple pipeline:

```yaml
name: Simple CI/CD

on:
  push:
    branches: [ main ]

jobs:
  build:
    runs-on: ubuntu-latest
    steps:
      - name: Checkout code
        uses: actions/checkout@v2

      - name: Build project
        run: echo "Building the application..."

      - name: Deploy
        run: echo "Deploying application..."
```

Push your code – the workflow will trigger automatically!
And just like that... you're using GitHub Actions!

Server Configuration with Ansible

What is Ansible?
Ansible is an open-source tool that lets you automate server setup and manage configuration easily.

Why Ansible?
- Agentless (no software needed on the server)
- Simple YAML syntax
- Great for automating repetitive tasks

Example: Installing Nginx with Ansible
1. Install Ansible on your control machine:

```
sudo apt update
sudo apt install ansible -y
```

Create an inventory file (e.g., hosts.ini):

```
[web]
your-ec2-ip ansible_user=ubuntu
ansible_ssh_private_key_file=/path/to/your-key.pem
```

Create a simple playbook (e.g., install-nginx.yml):

```yaml
- hosts: web
  become: yes
  tasks:
    - name: Install Nginx
      apt:
        name: nginx
        state: present
        update_cache: yes

    - name: Start Nginx
      service:
        name: nginx
        state: started
```

Run the playbook:

```
ansible-playbook -i hosts.ini install-nginx.yml
```

Boom! Your server is now running Nginx – all automated by Ansible.

Chapter Summary

- Automation saves time and reduces errors.
- CI/CD helps you deliver better software faster.
- Jenkins and GitHub Actions are great tools to automate builds and deployments.
- Ansible makes configuring servers a breeze.

Practical Challenge

⬛ Set up a basic Jenkins server and create a working pipeline.

⬛ Create a GitHub Actions workflow for one of your projects.

⬛ Write an Ansible playbook that installs and configures a basic web server.

The more you practice, the more second nature DevOps will become.

Chapter 7

Now that you've built a solid foundation, it's time to go beyond basics — into the real-world skills that separate junior engineers from true professionals.

This chapter will help you:
- Strengthen your security practices
- Build your own complete DevOps project
- Learn how to troubleshoot like a pro
- See the clear roadmap for growing your career

Let's dive deeper!

Security Best Practices in AWS

Security is not optional in DevOps.

Poor security can crash businesses – and end careers.
Here are essential AWS security practices every DevOps engineer must know:

1. Use IAM Roles and Policies Wisely

- Least Privilege: Always give users and applications only the permissions they absolutely need – nothing more.
- IAM Roles for EC2: Instead of embedding access keys into servers, assign IAM Roles to EC2 instances for safer access to AWS services.

2. Encrypt Data

- At Rest: Enable server-side encryption for data stored in S3 buckets, EBS volumes, and RDS databases.

In Transit: Always use HTTPS, SSL/TLS for data moving across the network.

3. Rotate Access Keys Regularly
- Never hard-code keys into your code.
- Use Secrets Manager or Parameter Store for sensitive information.

4. Use Multi-Factor Authentication (MFA)
- Enforce MFA for root accounts and important users.

5. Monitor and Audit
- Set up CloudTrail to record API activity.
- Use CloudWatch Alarms for suspicious activities.

Pro Tip: Security isn't a "one-time setup" — it's a daily habit.

Building Your Own DevOps Project (End-to-End Example)

Here's a real-world mini project you can build right now!

Project: Deploy a Web Application Using EC2, Git, Docker, and CI/CD

Step 1: Launch Infrastructure

- Create an EC2 instance (Ubuntu).
- Open port 80 (HTTP) and 22 (SSH) in the security group.

Step 2: Set Up Git

- Install Git.
- Clone your web application repo from GitHub.

Step 3: Containerize with Docker

- Write a Dockerfile for your app.
- Build and run your container.

Step 4: Set Up CI/CD

- Use GitHub Actions:
  - On code push   automatically SSH into EC2
  - Pull latest code   Build   Restart Docker container

Step 5: Monitor and Secure

- Set up basic CloudWatch alarms for CPU/memory.
- Enable logging for Docker containers.

You now have:

- Version control
- Continuous deployment
- Containerization
- Basic monitoring
- Security best practices

Congratulations – that's a real DevOps workflow!

Troubleshooting and Debugging Tips

Troubleshooting is a huge part of DevOps.

Here are practical tips that save real-world engineers every day:

1. Check Logs First
- Always check logs!
  - cat /var/log/syslog
  - docker logs <container_id>
  - CloudWatch logs for AWS services.

2. Divide and Conquer
- Break the system down into pieces: network   server application   database.

3. Use Linux Diagnostic Tools
- top, htop, netstat, iftop, df -h, free -m – learn these!

4. Stay Calm
- Panic breaks systems faster than bugs do.
- Slow down, document what's happening, and work logically.

Remember: Troubleshooting is a skill you build through experience, not a talent you're born with.

Career Roadmap: How to Grow as a DevOps Engineer
You've started your DevOps journey — but where does it lead?

Here's a realistic growth roadmap:

1. Junior DevOps Engineer
- Focus: Linux, Git, AWS basics, scripting (Bash, Python), Docker basics
- Certifications: AWS Cloud Practitioner or Solutions Architect – Associate

2. Mid-Level DevOps Engineer
- Focus: Advanced AWS services (VPC, Auto Scaling, Load Balancers), Terraform, CI/CD pipelines, monitoring/logging, security
- Certifications: AWS Certified DevOps Engineer – Professional

3. Senior DevOps Engineer / Site Reliability Engineer (SRE)
   - Focus: Large scale systems, Kubernetes, multi-cloud (AWS, GCP, Azure), cost optimization, resilience, architecture design
4. DevOps Architect / Engineering Manager
   - Focus: Leading teams, designing DevOps workflows across an organization, governance, compliance, budgets

Final Advice for Your DevOps Journey

- Stay hands-on: Lab practice beats theory every time.
- Keep learning: Cloud services and tools evolve fast.
- Build a portfolio: Showcase projects you've completed.
- Network: Join LinkedIn groups, Slack communities, and local meetups.
- Enjoy the ride: DevOps is an amazing, high-demand field – and you're already on your way!

Great job reaching this advanced stage.
 Let's move forward – bigger projects, bigger wins, and a brighter future ahead!

Quick Summary:

You now have a full professional chapter that:
- Is clear and motivating ■
- Provides real-world value ■
- Has a project readers can immediately do ■
- Shows a clear career growth path ■

Appendix: Bonus Resources

Congratulations on reaching this far!

As a bonus, I've included some extra resources to help you continue your DevOps journey beyond this book.

This appendix covers:

- DevOps and AWS Interview Questions and Sample Answers
- A Study Plan for earning your AWS Certifications
- Useful Links, Cheat Sheets, and Tools you'll want to bookmark

Let's dive in!

Here are common DevOps and AWS interview questions – with simple, clear answers you can practice:

1. What is DevOps?
Answer:

DevOps is a set of practices that combines software development (Dev) and IT operations (Ops).

It aims to shorten the development lifecycle and deliver high-quality software continuously.

2. What are the benefits of using Infrastructure as Code (IaC)?
Answer:
- Faster provisioning of resources
- Consistency across environments
- Easier version control of infrastructure
- Automated deployments

3. Explain the difference between Continuous Integration (CI) and Continuous Deployment (CD).
Answer:
- CI (Continuous Integration): Developers frequently merge code changes into a shared repository where builds and tests run automatically.
- CD (Continuous Deployment): Every code change that passes automated tests is automatically deployed to production.

4. What is a VPC in AWS?

Answer:

A VPC (Virtual Private Cloud) is a private network within AWS where you can launch resources like EC2 instances, databases, and load balancers — isolated from the public cloud but customizable.

5. How does Auto Scaling work in AWS?

Answer:

Auto Scaling automatically adjusts the number of EC2 instances based on traffic or demand. It helps maintain application availability and can lower costs by scaling down during low demand.

Tip: Practice answering these questions out loud in your own words to sound confident during interviews!

If you want to get AWS Certified, here's a suggested study path:

Phase 1: AWS Certified Cloud Practitioner (Foundational – Beginner)

- Learn basics: EC2, S3, IAM, CloudWatch, Pricing Models
- Recommended Time: 2–3 weeks (1 hour/day)

Phase 2: AWS Certified Solutions Architect – Associate (Core for DevOps)

- Focus on: VPC, ELB, Auto Scaling, CloudFormation, RDS, Route 53
- Recommended Time: 6–8 weeks (1–2 hours/day)
- Hands-On Labs: Launch EC2 instances, set up load balancers, create S3 buckets

Phase 3: AWS Certified DevOps Engineer – Professional (Advanced)

- Topics: CI/CD pipelines, Monitoring, Security, Automation (CloudFormation, CodePipeline, CodeDeploy)
- Recommended Time: 8–12 weeks (2 hours/day)

Useful Links and Cheat Sheets

Here's a curated list of tools and resources to help you master DevOps:

Learning Platforms

- AWS Free Tier – https://aws.amazon.com/free
- Katacoda (DevOps Scenarios) – https://www.katacoda.com
- Linux Academy / A Cloud Guru – Great for cloud certifications

Cheat Sheets

- Git Cheat Sheet – https://education.github.com/git-cheat-sheet-education.pdf
- AWS CLI Cheat Sheet – https://docs.aws.amazon.com/cli/latest/reference/index.html
- Linux Commands Cheat Sheet – https://www.gnu.org/software/bash/manual/bash.html

Useful Links and Cheat Sheets

Hands-On Practice
- AWS Hands-On Tutorials – https://aws.amazon.com/getting-started/hands-on
- Play With Docker (free online Docker labs) – https://labs.play-with-docker.com/

Documentation You Should Bookmark
- AWS Official Docs – https://docs.aws.amazon.com/
- Terraform Documentation – https://developer.hashicorp.com/terraform/docs
- Docker Documentation – https://docs.docker.com/

Remember: DevOps is a journey, not a sprint.
Stay consistent. Practice regularly.

Challenge yourself with small projects — and keep growing.
The tech world needs people like you: builders, doers, creators.
Keep pushing. Your DevOps future is just getting started!

www.ingramcontent.com/pod-product-compliance
Lightning Source LLC
LaVergne TN
LVHW081801050326
832903LV00027B/2042

* 9 7 9 8 2 8 0 6 6 3 2 7 5 *